5/28/88

To Emily
With a lot of love
and all best wishes
for a long and prosperous
life.
Love Aunt Nancy &
Uncle Clint

P.S. Happy Birthday!

# My First
# BIBLE
# WORD BOOK

By Yvonne S. Russell
Illustrated by June Goldsborough

**Rand McNally & Company**
Chicago • New York • San Francisco

Library of Congress Cataloging in Publication Data

Russell, Yvonne.
My first Bible word book.

Summary: Selected stories from the Old and New Testaments, each with an accompanying word matching activity.

1. Bible stories, English. [1. Bible stories.
2. Vocabulary] I. Goldsborough, June, ill. II. Title.
BS551.2.R8   1983        220.9'505        83–9557
ISBN 0–528–82421–X

First printing, 1983

## A Word to Parents and Teachers

Children love Bible stories—stories of heroes and mighty deeds, and of Jesus, the Son of God, born in a stable.

But children are full of questions, too.

"What is an ark?"

"Is that man in the picture David?"

"What is a manger?"

My *First Bible Word Book* is a book of stories and pictures, and more. Words—over 300 unique to the Bible stories—are printed on the pictures and again in a list accompanying the text. A child can match Bible words such as *unleavened bread, Passover Lamb, frankincense,* and a *sheep* lost and rescued by an anxious *shepherd* to these words in the illustrations. The words appear in the typeface teachers favor for the early grades.

My *First Bible Word Book* is designed for adult and child to use together during story time, then for the child to explore alone or with minimal assistance. Twenty-five stories from the Old and New Testaments depict the most vivid Bible scenes. God's creation, Noah, Joseph, and Moses the Lawgiver are here. Heroes David and Daniel stand fast in the face of danger. Jesus is born, heralded by angels; he teaches and performs mighty miracles; he dies, but lives again and ascends to heaven. The pictures will draw children again and again to *see* the Bible story, and to find a word missed the last time.

Matching the words allows a child to actively participate in learning Bible truths at an early age. With this in mind, read a story aloud. Assist the child in matching the words. Then let the child explore and enjoy on his or her own.

This book is dedicated to my parents and to the many Sunday School and Bible teachers who loved and guided me over the years.

My thanks, too, to Elsie McCall, early childhood education specialist, for her review and valuable comments concerning the word list.

Yvonne Russell

Darkness

Star

Land

# CONTENTS

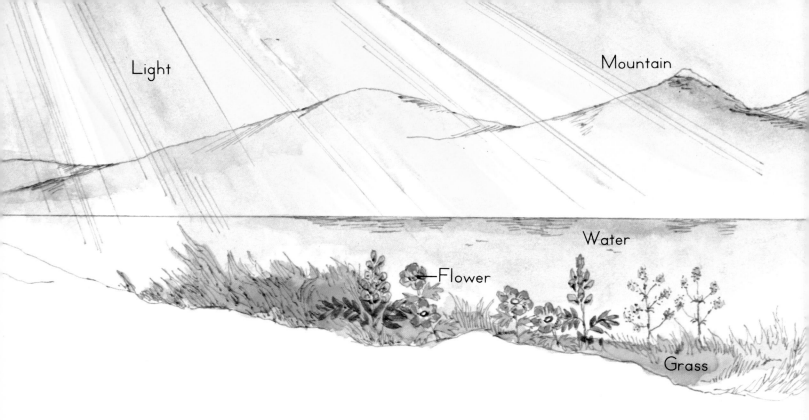

Light

Mountain

Water

Flower

Grass

## God Makes Heaven and Earth

In the beginning God made the heavens and the earth. At first the earth had no shape and was empty and dark.

But God said, "Let there be light," and there was light. God called the light day and the darkness night. This was the first day.

On the second day, God made the sky and called it the heavens. On the third day, He made the waters come together and the dry land appear. God called the land earth and the waters seas. "Let all kinds of plants, grass, and trees grow on the land," He said. And plants grew, with flowers and fruit and seeds.

On the fourth day, God said, "Let there be lights in the sky." So the sun and moon and stars appeared.

On the fifth day, God made every kind of fish and filled the sky with birds.

On the sixth day, God made every kind of animal: running and

10

jumping animals, creeping and crawling animals. Then He said, "Let us make man in our likeness." So God made man and woman and blessed them.

God was pleased with everything He had made. Then, on the seventh day, He rested from His work.

## Match these words with the words in the picture:

| | | | |
|---|---|---|---|
| Heavens | Seas | Elephant | Walrus |
| Sun | Earth | Plant | Flower |
| Moon | Bird | Man | Frog |
| Tree | Dry Land | Woman | Giraffe |
| Fish | Lion | Grass | Caterpillar |
| Whale | | | |

## Adam and Eve

God made man and woman to live in the world. Their names were Adam and Eve. God put them in a beautiful garden, called Eden, that had two special trees—the Tree of Life and the Tree of Knowledge of Good and Evil. God said to Adam, "If you eat the fruit of the Tree of Knowledge of Good and Evil, you will die."

Now the serpent, the slyest creature God had made, tricked Eve. "If you eat the fruit of the Tree of Knowledge of Good and Evil, you will not die. You will become as wise as God," he said.

Eve believed the serpent. She ate the fruit and gave some to Adam. They both knew they had disobeyed God.

When God visited Eden, Adam and Eve hid from Him. God called to Adam, "Why are you hiding? Did you eat the fruit I warned you about?"

"Yes," said Adam, "Eve gave it to me."

"I was tricked by the serpent," said Eve.

So God cursed the serpent. Forever after he would crawl on the ground, and people would hate him. Then God drove Adam and Eve out of Eden. Mighty angels barred the way so they could never go back, and a flaming sword guarded the Tree of Life.

**Match these words with the words in the picture:**

| | | |
|---|---|---|
| Adam | Flaming Sword | Garden of Eden |
| Angel | Fruit | Tree of Knowledge of |
| Bush | Butterfly | Good and Evil |
| Eve | Tree of Life | |
| Tree | Serpent | |

## Noah's Ark

Many, many years passed after Adam and Eve left the Garden of Eden. People became so wicked that God decided to destroy all living things.

But Noah was good, and God loved him. God said to Noah, "Build a huge boat, an ark, of gopher wood. Fill it with food and two of each kind of animal, for I am going to destroy all life on earth."

Noah built the ark and took his three sons—Ham, Shem, and Japheth—their wives, and the animals into it. Then God, Himself, shut the door.

Rain fell forty days and nights and covered all the earth, even the mountains, with water. Only Noah and his family were safe, afloat in the ark.

At last the storm ended, and a wind dried the flood. The ark came to rest on Mount Ararat, and Noah sent a raven and a dove to find land. When the earth was dry, God told Noah he and his family could leave the ark with the animals and begin to build their homes and plant their gardens.

Then God made a promise: "Never again will I destroy the whole earth with a flood," He said. "My rainbow will remind you of My promise."

**Match these words with the words in the picture:**

| | | |
|---|---|---|
| Noah | Mount Ararat | Hippopotamus |
| Ham | Raven | Pig |
| Shem | Dove | Gopher Wood |
| Japheth | Camel | Dog |
| Noah's Wife | Crocodile | Chicken |
| Ark | Tiger | Goose |
| Rain | Goat | Elephant |

Land of Canaan

Milk

Meat

Bread

Butter

Water Jug

Servant

Visitor

## Abraham and Sarah Have a Son

Now God chose Abraham to be the father of a great nation and promised him the land of Canaan for his own land. But Abraham and his wife Sarah were old and had no children.

One day three men appeared to Abraham as he sat under an oak tree. Abraham welcomed them and invited them to rest and eat. Servants brought water for washing, while Sarah cooked bread. Abraham set meat, butter, and fresh milk before his guests.

After they finished eating, one of the strangers asked, "Where is Sarah?"

"In the tent," replied Abraham.

"I shall come back to see you next year, and Sarah will have a son then," said the visitor.

Tent

Oak Tree

Sarah

Abraham

Sarah was in the tent listening, and she laughed when she heard what the visitor said. She did not believe him.

The visitor asked Abraham, "Why did Sarah laugh? Is anything too hard for the Lord? When I come back, Sarah shall have a son."

The next year, when she was ninety years old, Sarah had a baby boy. She named him *Isaac*, which means "laughter."

Isaac's son Israel would become the father of a great nation—the nation of the Israelites.

## Match these words with the words in the picture:

| | | |
|---|---|---|
| Abraham | Bread | Oak Tree |
| Sarah | Meat | Butter |
| Tent | Servant | Milk |
| Visitor | Water Jug | Land of Canaan |

## Joseph's Story

Israel had twelve sons. To one, Joseph, he gave a coat of many colors. The other sons grew jealous and sold their brother as a slave to a caravan of Midianite traders bound for Egypt.

One night, Pharaoh—king of Egypt—dreamed a strange dream. Joseph was called to him, because Joseph could tell the meanings of dreams.

"A terrible famine is coming," said Joseph. "You, O King, must store grain to feed the people."

Pharaoh put Joseph in charge of the grain. When famine came, the storehouses of Egypt were full. But in Canaan the people were hungry. Israel sent his ten oldest sons to Egypt to buy food.

Joseph's brothers did not know him, so he decided to test them.

"You are spies, are you not?" he said.

"Oh no, sir," they cried. "We are twelve brothers, the sons of one man. The youngest son is at home, the other disappeared long ago."

"If this is true," said Joseph, "bring me this youngest son. Then will I believe you."

So the brothers brought young Benjamin to Egypt. As they sat with Joseph, he quietly ordered his favorite silver cup hidden in Benjamin's grain sack. When his brothers left, Joseph sent his steward to search their donkey packs. There, in Benjamin's sack, was the missing cup!

The frightened brothers were brought once more before Joseph. To their surprise, he hugged each one of them.

"Don't you know me?" he cried. "I am your brother Joseph. Go now and bring our father to me."

The brothers joyfully brought Israel and all their families to Egypt, and there they lived for many years.

## Match these words with the words in the picture:

| | | |
|---|---|---|
| Joseph in Canaan | Caravan | Grain Sack |
| Coat of Many Colors | Slave | Storehouse |
| Joseph's Brothers | Steward | Grain |
| Midianite Trader | Silver Cup | |
| Joseph in Egypt | Benjamin | |

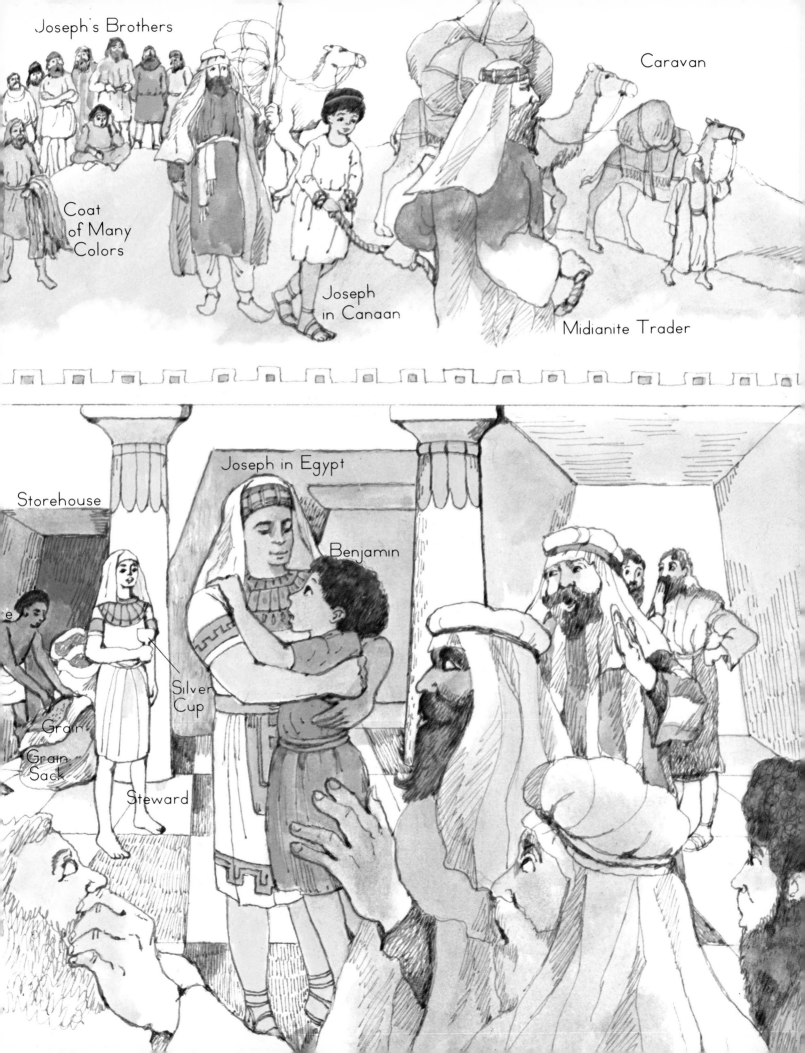

Joseph's Brothers

Caravan

Coat
of Many
Colors

Joseph
in Canaan

Midianite Trader

Storehouse

Joseph in Egypt

Benjamin

Silver
Cup

Grain

Grain
Sack

Steward

## Baby Moses

Many, many years passed after Joseph invited his brothers and their families, the Israelites, to live in Egypt during the famine. An evil king, a new Pharaoh, made slaves of the Israelites and ordered his soldiers to kill all the Israelite boy babies.

One Israelite mother, named Jochebed, hid her baby from the soldiers for three months. Then she built a little basket of reeds, put the baby in it, and set it among the bulrushes by the River Nile. The baby's sister Miriam hid herself and watched to see what would happen.

The Pharaoh's daughter and her maids came down to the river to bathe. This princess saw the little boat and looked inside. What did she see? A tiny baby crying.

Miriam ran forward and bowed to Pharaoh's daughter.

"Would you like me to find someone to care for the baby?" she asked.

"Yes," replied the royal lady.

So Miriam ran home and returned with Jochebed, the baby's mother.

The princess commanded, "Take care of this baby for me, and I will pay you."

So Jochebed cared for her baby, her own baby. The princess named him *Moses*, which means "to draw out," because she drew him out of the river. And Moses grew up a prince in Egypt.

## Match these words with the words in the picture:

| | | |
|---|---|---|
| Handmaiden | Palm Tree | Bulrush |
| Baby Moses | Miriam | River Nile |
| Reed Basket | Jochebed | Palace |
| Pharaoh's Daughter | Egypt | |

Egypt

Palm Tree

Palace

Jochebed

Miriam

Handmaiden

Pharaoh's Daughter

Baby Moses

Bulrush

Reed Basket

River Nile

## Moses Leads the Israelites out of Egypt

When Moses grew up, he angered Pharaoh, who ordered him killed. So Moses ran away to the land of Midian and became a shepherd.

One day, as Moses watched the sheep, God called to him.

"Moses, Moses," He said, "I have heard the cry of My people. Go to Pharaoh and tell him to set them free."

Moses went before Pharaoh. "Let the Israelites go," he said.

"Never!" shouted Pharaoh.

So Moses threw his staff upon the ground. It became a slithering serpent. Then he changed the River Nile to blood. He caused frogs to cover the land and changed dust into tiny, itching, biting, gnats. Swarms of pesky flies appeared. The cattle became sick, and sores broke out on the skin of the Egyptians. Hail, locusts, and darkness covered Egypt, but still, Pharaoh would not let the people go.

Finally, God commanded Moses, "Tell each Israelite family to roast a lamb, eat it, and put its blood on the doorposts of their house. This sign will keep them safe from what I shall do."

At midnight, the Angel of Death passed over the houses of the

Israelites, but in every Egyptian house, the oldest son died.

"Leave!" Pharaoh begged at last. "Take all the Israelites and leave."

So the people took their cattle, their sheep, and unleavened bread to eat, and they left Egypt.

Soon Pharaoh changed his mind. He sent his army in chariots charging after the Israelites to the shores of the Red Sea. But God parted the waters, and the people walked across on dry land.

The Egyptians plunged after them, but now God let the walls of water go, and the soldiers were drowned. The children of Israel were free at last.

## Match these words with the words in the picture:

| | | |
|---|---|---|
| Moses | Lamb | Chariot |
| Pharaoh | Unleavened Bread | Israelite |
| Staff | Wall of Water | |
| Red Sea | Egyptian Army | |

# The Ten Commandments

Moses led the Israelites out of Egypt and they wandered in the wilderness until they came to Mount Sinai. God called to Moses.

"Tell the people to stay at the foot of the mountain," He said.

Thunder rolled and the mountain shook, and the people watched Moses enter the black, smoking cloud that hung over the mountain. Moses left his brother Aaron to care for the people.

For forty days and forty nights, Moses was hidden behind the cloud. Then God Himself wrote Ten Commandments on tablets of stone. These were rules that told the people what they should and should not do, what was right and what was wrong.

Moses carefully took the tablets and carried them down the mountain. But when he saw the people, Moses was angry. The Israelites were not praying to God. They were praying to a golden calf, an *idol,* they had made. Moses threw the tablets on the ground and broke them.

"What have you done, Aaron?" he asked his brother. "Why have you brought this sin on the people?"

"You were gone so long, the people thought you were not coming back," said Aaron. "They were afraid, and they asked me to make a god to lead them."

Moses punished those who had worshipped the idol. Then he returned to the mountain. God was angry with the Israelites, but at last He forgave them. Moses again received the Ten Commandments and brought them to the people.

## Match these words with the words in the picture:

| | | |
|---|---|---|
| Moses | Smoke | Mount Sinai |
| Aaron | Israelites | Ten Commandments |
| Idol | Tablet | Altar |
| Cloud | Golden Calf | Wilderness |

Ten Commandments

Moses

Cloud

Wilderness

Mount Sinai

Israelites

Smoke

Golden Calf

Idol

Altar

Aaron

Tablet

# David and Goliath

After the Israelites settled in their own land, they were attacked by the Philistines, who lived nearby. The Israelites and their king Saul fought hard, but the Philistines were strong.

Now David was a young man who took care of his father's sheep. One day, his father told him to take some food to his brothers in the Israelite army.

When David arrived, he greeted his brothers; but suddenly their talk stopped. Out of the Philistine camp stepped a giant. He walked back and forth before them, shaking his spear and shouting.

"Who is that?" David asked.

"That is Goliath, the Philistine giant," said the soldiers. "King Saul will reward anyone who defeats him."

Everyone was surprised when David, young David, stepped onto the battlefield. He wore no sword or armor. His only weapons were a shepherd's staff, a sling, and five smooth stones.

When Goliath saw David, he roared, "Do you think I am a dog that you fight me with a stick? Come here and I will tear you up!"

David shouted back so all the army could hear, "You attack me with a sword and spear, but I attack you in the name of the Lord."

David put a stone in his sling, whirled it around, then threw it. The stone hit Goliath in the forehead, and he fell to the ground dead. Then David grabbed Goliath's sword and cut off the giant's head.

And that is how David defeated Goliath, with a sling, a stone, and faith in God.

## Match these words with the words in the picture:

| | | |
|---|---|---|
| Armor | Philistine Soldier | Shield |
| David | Israelite Soldier | Sword |
| Goliath | Shepherd's Staff | Spear |
| Helmet | Smooth Stones | Army |
| King Saul | Sling | |

## Daniel in the Lions' Den

After many years, God allowed His people to be captured by their enemies and taken to Babylon far away. One Israelite, named Daniel, became a friend of Darius, king of Babylon, and helped to rule the kingdom. The other counselors were jealous and plotted against Daniel; but the king trusted his friend, and the plots failed.

"There must be some way to trap this Daniel," thought the counselors, these satraps of Babylon. They made a plan.

"King, we know you are as great as a god," they said. "Make a law and sign it, saying all must pray to you, and only you, or be thrown into the lions' den."

The king was pleased to think himself a god, so he signed the law. Then the counselors watched Daniel to see whom he would worship. Of course, Daniel worshipped God, not the king.

"King Darius," said the counselors, "did you not sign a law that all your subjects must worship you, and only you?"

"I did," replied the king.

"Then Daniel has disobeyed the law," they shouted, "for he worships *his* God and not the king."

Darius tried to think of ways to save Daniel, but the law could not be changed. That night, Daniel was lowered into the lions' den.

In the morning, Darius rushed to the pit. "Daniel, Daniel!" he cried. "Did your God save you?"

"God sent His angel to close the lions' mouths. They have not hurt me," Daniel called.

With great joy, Darius lifted Daniel from the pit. Then he ordered the three wicked satraps thrown in instead. And Daniel's God was proclaimed throughout the land.

**Match these words with the words in the picture:**

| | | |
|---|---|---|
| Daniel | King Darius | Boulder |
| Lions' Den | Satrap | Chain |
| Lion | Rope | Babylon |

Satrap

King Darius

Babylon

Boulder

Daniel

Lion

Rope

Chain

Lions' Den

Stable

Donkey

Joseph

Baby
Jesus

Swaddling
Clothes

Manger

Mary

Straw

Lamb

Shepherd

## Jesus Is Born

Many, many years passed. The Israelites—now called Jews—left Babylon and returned to their own land. But the Romans, a powerful people, soon came and ruled over them. The Jews prayed and prayed for a Messiah, or Savior, to set them free. At last, God answered their prayers. He sent his angel Gabriel to visit Mary, a young woman living in Nazareth.

"The Lord is with you, Mary. Do not be afraid," said Gabriel. "You will have a baby boy and He shall be called the Son of God."

Mary was surprised, but she answered quietly, "I will do what God wishes. May everything you say come true."

Joseph, who was engaged to Mary, heard that she would soon have a baby. *How can this be?* he wondered. Troubled, Joseph fell asleep. An angel spoke to him in a dream.

"Joseph, do not be afraid to become Mary's husband," said the angel. "Mary's child is the Son of God. You shall name Him Jesus, because He will save people from their sins."

So Joseph took Mary home and they were married.

About this time, Caesar Augustus—the Roman emperor—ordered everyone to journey to the town of their fathers to pay a special tax. Joseph went to Bethlehem, the City of David, because

Bethlehem

Inn

Angel

he came from the family of David. He took Mary with him.

While they were there, the time came for Mary's baby to be born. There was no room in the inn, so the baby was born in a stable. Mary gently wrapped him in swaddling clothes and laid him in a manger.

Nearby, shepherds were watching their sheep. An angel appeared to them. "I bring wonderful news!" said the angel. "Tonight the Savior is born in Bethlehem. You will find Him lying in a manger."

The shepherds found Joseph, Mary, and baby Jesus in Bethlehem, just as the angel had said. They joyfully told the good news to all they met, but Mary kept these things quietly in her heart.

## Match these words with the words in the picture:

| | | |
|---|---|---|
| Stable | Baby Jesus | Inn |
| Manger | Lamb | Swaddling Clothes |
| Mary | Straw | Angel |
| Joseph | Donkey | |
| Shepherd | Bethlehem | |

## The Three Wise Men Visit Jesus

Wicked Herod was king of Judea, where Jesus was born.

One day, three wise men arrived in Jerusalem. "Where is the newborn king of the Jews?" they asked. "We have seen his star in the East and have come to worship him."

King Herod heard of the strangers and was worried. Was not he himself the king of the Jews? Who was this child they spoke of? Herod decided to find out. He gathered all the chief priests and scribes and asked, "Who is this king of the Jews and where can he be found?"

"He is the Messiah," they replied, "and He will be born in Bethlehem."

Then Herod, wicked Herod, called the three wise men to him. "When you find this new king, come and tell me so I may worship him too," he said.

Once more the star appeared in the East, and the wise men followed it until they stood before a small house. The star flickered above them. Mary welcomed them in, and their hearts filled with joy. They bowed low before the child Jesus and gave him presents of gold and frankincense and myrrh.

When the three prepared to leave, God warned them in a dream not to return to Herod. They departed to their own land another way.

Now the angel of the Lord appeared to Joseph and said, "Take the baby from here quickly, for King Herod will soon try to kill him."

Joseph left that same night, taking Mary and Jesus to Egypt.

Just as the angel had said, Herod ordered all the boy babies in Bethlehem killed. But Jesus was not there; he was safe.

Later, after wicked Herod died, Joseph brought Jesus and Mary back to Israel, and they lived in Nazareth.

## Match these words with the words in the picture:

| | | |
|---|---|---|
| House | Joseph | First Wise Man |
| Mary | Gold | Second Wise Man |
| Jesus | Frankincense | Third Wise Man |
| Star | Myrrh | |
| Bethlehem | Lamp | |

## The Boy Jesus in the Temple

When Jesus was twelve years old, he left Nazareth and journeyed with Mary and Joseph to Jerusalem for the wonderful Passover feast. The holy city was bustling with Jews from many strange lands—Jesus had never seen so much excitement.

When the holiday was over, Mary and Joseph started home. At first, they did not know that Jesus was missing. They thought he was with their friends behind them on the road. But when night came, they could not find their son, so they rushed back to the crowded city to look for him.

Three days passed. Tired and worried, Mary and Joseph finally found Jesus in the temple, talking with the teachers there. All the teachers were amazed how well young Jesus understood the Law.

Mary and Joseph were happy to find Jesus, but upset too. "My son, why have you done this to us?" asked Mary. "We have searched for you everywhere."

"But why did you need to search?" Jesus asked. "Did you not know I would be here in my Father's house?"

Joseph and Mary did not understand what their son meant.

Jesus returned to Nazareth and was a good son to Mary and Joseph. He grew tall and wise and was loved by God and by all the people he met.

## Match these words with the words in the picture:

| | | |
|---|---|---|
| Jesus | Prayer Shawl | Temple |
| Teacher | Bench | Scroll |
| Scribe | Mary | Chest |
| Robe | Joseph | |

John the Baptist

Spirit of God

Heaven

Jordan River

Leather Girdle

Water

Coat of Camel's Hair

Baptism

Jesus

## Jesus Is Baptized

John the Baptist was Jesus' cousin. He lived in the desert and, like prophets of old, wore a coat of rough camel's hair and a leather girdle, or belt. John heard God's word and began preaching beside the River Jordan.

"Be baptized to show you have turned to God," John warned the people. "Turn away from your sins, and you will be forgiven."

People listened to John—villagers, farmers, soldiers came to him. Even tax collectors who cheated the people came to John to be baptized.

There were some who demanded of John, "Do you claim to be the Messiah, or Christ?"

"No," he said, "I am not the Christ."

"Then who are you?" they asked. "What right have you to baptize?"

John answered, "I baptize only with water, but someone is coming who is greater than I. He will baptize you with the Holy Spirit and with fire."

36

Then one day, John saw Jesus, and John said to the people, "Look! There is the Lamb of God I told you about, He who takes away the sin of the world!"

After the crowds were baptized, Jesus turned to John and said, "Baptize me also." So Jesus was baptized. And he came out of the water, praying. Suddenly, the heavens opened, and the Holy Spirit in the form of a dove came down upon Jesus. A voice from heaven spoke: "You are My beloved Son. With you I am well pleased."

And John saw this and said, "Truly He is the Son of God."

**Match these words with the words in the picture:**

| | | |
|---|---|---|
| Jordan River | Jesus | Water |
| John the Baptist | Baptism | Desert |
| Coat of Camel's Hair | Spirit of God | Villager |
| Leather Girdle | Tax Collector | Farmer |
| Sandal | Heaven | Soldier |

Jesus

Andrew

Peter

Capernaum

Fish

Net

## Men Who Followed Jesus

After Jesus was baptized, he went into the wilderness where he remained for forty days. Then he traveled to Capernaum, beside the Sea of Galilee, there to begin preaching the good news of God's kingdom.

One day, Jesus saw a fisherman, named Peter, standing beside a boat. "Take me out to sea and let down your nets," said Jesus.

"I will do as you say," said Peter, "but there are no fish today. We fished all night and caught nothing."

But as soon as the nets were let down, they were filled to bursting with fish! Peter called to his brother Andrew to help with the nets. Then they called James and John, brothers also, to help.

"Do not be afraid," said Jesus to Peter. "Soon you will be catching men, not fish."

In all, Jesus chose twelve to be his disciples. Peter, Andrew, James, John, Philip, Bartholomew, Thomas, Matthew, James the son of Alphaeus, Judas the son of James, Simon the Zealot, and Judas Iscariot—these men followed Jesus wherever he went, learning

from him, seeing his miracles, watching him heal the sick and raise the dead.

Later, the Twelve went among those who had not known Jesus and brought them the good news: The Messiah had come at last to bring the people back to God!

## Match these words with the words in the picture:

| | | |
|---|---|---|
| Peter | Net | Oar |
| Andrew | Jesus | Fish |
| James | Sea of Galilee | Fisherman |
| John | Capernaum | |
| Fishing Boat | Sail | |

## Mary and Martha

One day, Jesus and his disciples traveled to Jerusalem. On the way, they stopped at Bethany to visit good friends—Mary and Martha and their brother Lazarus—for Jesus loved this family very much.

As they were talking, Mary sat on the floor, listening to everything Jesus said; but Martha was weighted down with care. She scurried back and forth, clattering dishes and worrying about the big dinner she was cooking for the guests.

"Master," Martha complained, "do you not think it is wrong for my sister to just sit here while I do all the work? Tell her to help me."

But Jesus said to her, "Martha, Martha, you are fussing over little things. Only one thing is really important, and Mary has chosen it. I shall not take it away from her!"

Another time Jesus visited, and the family prepared a banquet in his honor. While everyone was eating, Mary took a jar of nard, a costly perfume, and knelt before Jesus. Gently, she poured every last drop over his feet, wiping them clean with her hair. The whole house was filled with the lovely smell.

But Judas Iscariot, who carried the disciples' money bag, frowned. "How wasteful!" he exclaimed. "Why was that perfume not sold and the money given to the poor?"

Jesus could see the bad thoughts in Judas' heart. "Let her alone, Judas," he said. "She did it for me. You will always have poor people who need help, but I shall not be with you for very long." For Jesus loved his friends, who showed him so much love.

**Match these words with the words in the picture:**

| | | |
|---|---|---|
| Mary | Dish | Money Bag |
| Martha | Perfume | Bethany |
| Lazarus | Disciple | Jar |
| Judas Iscariot | Guest | Jesus |
| Table | Hair | |

## Children Come to Jesus

Jesus loved people and they loved him. Poor people loved him, and rich people loved him. Women drawing water from a well loved him, and fishermen of the sea loved him. Even tax collectors from the city loved him. All saw his power to heal sickness, and many came just to be near him and to touch him.

One day, some mothers brought their babies to Jesus for his blessing. But the disciples knew Jesus was tired, so they told the women to take the children away.

When Jesus saw this, he called the children and gathered them around him. Then he said to his disciples, "Always let children come to me! Never send them away! For my Father's kingdom belongs to those who trust Him like little children. Anyone who does not trust as a child does will never pass through the gates into His kingdom."

Another time, the disciples were arguing who among them would

Woman

Fisherman

Rich Woman

Tax Collector

Well

be most important in God's kingdom. Jesus heard their fighting and called a little child to stand beside him.

To his disciples he said, "Unless you become as trusting as this child, you will never come into the kingdom. He who trusts like a child shall be the greatest in the kingdom. For, whoever cares for a trusting child shows his love for me, and whoever loves me loves my Father who sent me. The way you love and care for others shows your love for God and how great you are in His kingdom."

**Match these words with the words in the picture:**

Jesus        Well            Blessing

Disciple     Tax Collector   Woman

Mother       Poor Man        Father

Baby         Rich Woman      Children

Child        Fisherman

## Jesus Heals a Sick Little Girl

One day, a man named Jairus struggled through the crowd around Jesus and the disciples. Jairus was an important man, a leader of the synagogue where people gathered to pray. He bowed low before Jesus.

"Please come, Master," he begged. "My little girl is dying. She is only twelve years old. If you come, you can heal her."

Jesus pushed his way past the people and followed Jairus.

Just then a messenger ran up. "Your daughter is dead, Jairus," he said. "It is too late. There is no need to ask the Master to come now."

When Jesus heard this, he turned to Jairus. "Do not be afraid," he said. "Trust me." And they pushed ahead through the crowd to the house.

When they arrived, Jesus took Jairus and Peter and James and John in with him. Everywhere, friends and relatives were weeping and moaning with grief.

Jesus said to them, "Stop your crying. The child is not dead. She is only asleep."

But the people knew she was dead. They did not believe Jesus.

Jesus and his three disciples went with Jairus and his wife into the little girl's room. Taking her limp, cold hand in his own, Jesus commanded, "Child, I say to you, get up."

The girl opened her eyes and sat up, well again.

"Now, give her something to eat!" Jesus said to her mother and father.

They were filled with joy to have their daughter back again and wanted to shout the news to everyone, but Jesus commanded them not to tell anyone what he had done.

## Match these words with the words in the picture:

| | | |
|---|---|---|
| Jesus | Mother | Shutter |
| Jairus | Bed | Broth |
| Little Girl | Grandmother | Meat |
| Peter | Grandfather | Bread |
| James | Friend | |
| John | Lamp | |

## Jesus Feeds Five Thousand

Wherever Jesus traveled, crowds followed him to see him heal the sick and the crippled and to hear his teachings. Even when he tried to be alone high in the hills above the Sea of Galilee, the people followed him—though this was far from home and they were poor and hungry.

Jesus looked out over the crowd. Then he turned to Philip, one of his disciples. "How can we buy enough food for all these people, Philip?" Jesus asked. This question was only a test, for Jesus already knew what he himself was about to do.

"Why, Master, even a great bag of gold would not buy enough food for everyone!" Philip replied.

Just then Andrew appeared with a young boy who was carrying a basket. "This boy has five barley loaves and two fish," said Andrew, "but not nearly enough to feed so many."

"Tell everyone to sit down," ordered Jesus. And the people—over five thousand of them—sat upon the soft grass.

Jesus next took the loaves—just five of them—and the two small fish, and he gave thanks to God. Then he passed the food among the people. Everyone ate and ate—all they could hold!

"Now," commanded Jesus, "collect the scraps." The disciples returned with twelve baskets filled to the brim with crusts of uneaten bread. Five thousand had eaten, and yet, food remained!

The people saw this miracle, how Jesus had fed them, and they shouted, "Jesus, be our king!" But Jesus knew this was not God's plan, so he slipped away into the mountains to be alone.

## Match these words with the words in the picture:

| Andrew | Hillside | Fish |
| Philip | Sea of Galilee | Jesus |
| Boy | Crowd | |
| Barley Loaf | Grass | |

Hillside

Crowd

Sea of Galilee

Barley
Loaf

Boy

Grass

Fish

Andrew

Philip

Jesus

Storm

Sheepfold

Staff

Torch

Hill

Neighbor

Friend    Campfire

Shepherd

## The Lost Sheep

The leaders of the people did not understand why Jesus spent so much time with sinners, thieves, even the tax collectors who were so hated. The leaders would not even let those people into their houses!

Jesus knew most of the people kept sheep. Sheep gave them wool and meat and could be sold for money to buy things. Many times the people gave the sheep names and loved them like children. So Jesus told the people this story:

"A man once owned a hundred sheep, but one of them strayed away and became lost in the wilderness. As he did every night, the man counted his sheep when they entered the gate of the sheepfold. When he saw that one was missing, he left the ninety-nine safely penned in the fold, and then he went out into the hills. In the storm and the darkness he searched for the lost one. He carried a staff in one hand, to fight off wolves, and a torch in the other, to light the

48

Wolf

Cliff

Wilderness

Lost Sheep

way. Finally he found his little sheep, and he joyfully carried it home on his shoulders.

"When the man returned to the campfire beside the sheepfold, he invited his friends and neighbors, the other shepherds, to celebrate with him because he had found his lost sheep.

"In the same way," Jesus said, "God is happier over one lost sinner who returns to Him than over ninety-nine others who haven't strayed away! For God loves everyone who comes to Him, no matter what that person has done."

## Match these words with the words in the picture:

| | | |
|---|---|---|
| Lost Sheep | Hill | Neighbor |
| Shepherd | Cliff | Storm |
| Wilderness | Torch | Staff |
| Sheepfold | Campfire | |
| Wolf | Friend | |

# The Prodigal Son

Jesus told this story to explain how God loves and welcomes us when we stray away and come back to Him.

"A man had two sons who one day would receive all the riches that he owned. But the younger son said, 'Father, give me my share of your property now, instead of later when you die!' So the man divided his property between his two sons.

"Soon his younger son packed up, took a pouch full of money, and left home for a distant land. There he lived wildly, spending all that he had, until not a penny was left.

"Now a great famine swept the land, and there was no food. Hungry and penniless, the young man went to a farmer, who hired him to feed his pigs. The young man became so hungry that even the pods the pigs ate looked good to him. Finally he came to his senses, thinking, 'At home even the servants have plenty of food. I shall go home and tell my father I have been a fool, sinning against God and against him. I shall ask him to let me work for him, not as his son, but as a servant.'

"So he returned home, weak and hungry. While he was still far off, his father saw him coming and ran down the road to meet him, kissing and hugging the young man joyfully.

"'Father,' said the boy, 'I have sinned against heaven and you. I am not worthy to be called your son—'

"But his father turned to the servants. 'Hurry!' he shouted. 'Bring the best robe and shoes. And a jeweled ring! Roast the fatted calf we have been saving for a feast. This son of mine was like one lost and dead to me, and now he is alive.' And so the feast began and all were happy."

## Match these words with the words in the picture:

| | | |
|---|---|---|
| Younger Son | Pouch | Shoe |
| Older Son | Robe | Fatted Calf |
| Father | Jeweled Ring | Feast |

Older Son

Feast

Fatted Calf

Robe

Pouch

Jeweled
Ring

Father

Shoe

Younger Son

Samaritan

Donkey

Wounded Man

Robe

Bandage

Wine

Sandal

## The Good Neighbor

A scribe, one who studied the Law, asked Jesus slyly, "What shall I do, Master, to live in heaven?"

"What does our Law say?" Jesus asked him.

"Love God above all and love your neighbor as much as yourself," the man replied.

"That is right," Jesus said.

"But which neighbors?" the scribe asked, for he and his friends disliked their neighbors, the Samaritans, and would not work or visit or eat with these people. So Jesus told this story:

"A man traveling to Jericho was attacked by robbers. They stole his money, even his clothes, then beat him half to death and left him lying beside the road.

"A priest of the temple walked by. When he saw the man, he crossed the road to avoid him and went on his way. A Levite, who worked in the temple, also passed by the man.

"Then a Samaritan came along. When he saw the wounded man, he helped him. Gently he poured oil and wine over the wounds and bandaged them. Then he carried the man on his donkey to an

inn and watched over him all night. The next morning, he gave the innkeeper money, saying, 'Take care of this man until he is well enough to travel. If it costs more than this, I shall pay you when I return.'"

Jesus turned to the scribe and asked, "Who was a neighbor to the wounded man?"

"The one who helped him," the scribe answered.

"Yes," said Jesus. "Now you do the same."

## Match these words with the words in the picture:

| | | |
|---|---|---|
| Wounded Man | Oil | Wine |
| Priest | Inn | Bandage |
| Levite | Robe | Innkeeper |
| Samaritan | Sandal | |
| Donkey | Jericho | |

Philip

James

John

Jesus

Unleavened
Bread

Towel

Thomas

Cup
of Wine

Matthew

Passover Lamb

## The Last Supper

It was time for the Passover festival. Jesus said to Peter and John, "Go to Jerusalem and you will meet a man carrying a jar of water. Follow him and you will find a house with a large upper room to make ready for the Passover feast."

So Peter and John went to Jerusalem and prepared the Passover supper of roast lamb and unleavened bread.

Later, all the disciples sat around the table. Quietly, Jesus rose and washed the feet of each of them, as a slave would, to show how each should serve the others. Then he took a loaf of unleavened bread, blessed it, and broke off a piece for each disciple, saying, "This is my body, given for you. Eat it to remember me."

Then he gave them wine, saying, "This cup is a sign of God's new promise. Soon I shall pour out my blood to save many souls. But one of you will betray me," and he turned to look at each one of them. "I must die; it is God's plan. But woe and horror await him who betrays me."

Quickly Judas Iscariot looked away. He remembered the coins in his pouch—thirty silver coins—which Jesus' enemies had paid him to help them trap Jesus.

Later that night Jesus walked alone outside the city, praying, in the Garden of Gethsemane. But Judas knew where Jesus could be found; in the darkness he led a great crowd—and the temple guards—to Jesus. The guards arrested Jesus, and he was brought before Pontius Pilate, the Roman governor.

At last, just as he himself had foretold, Jesus was sent to die on the cross to suffer for the sins of the world.

## Match these words with the words in the picture:

| | | |
|---|---|---|
| Jesus | Bartholomew | Judas Iscariot |
| Towel | Matthew | Passover Lamb |
| Silver Coin | Thomas | Unleavened Bread |
| Andrew | Peter | Simon the Zealot |
| James | John | James the Son of Alphaeus |
| Philip | Cup of Wine | Judas the Son of James |

# The Resurrection

When Jesus died on the cross, his sad friends stood watching from a distance, troubled and afraid. After a time, Joseph, a good man from the city of Arimathea, went to Pontius Pilate and asked him for Jesus' body. Gently, Joseph took Jesus down from the cross. He wrapped him in a clean linen shroud, or burial cloth, and laid him in a new tomb cut into solid rock. Finally, a great stone was rolled over the door, shutting the tomb tight.

Mary Magdalene and the other women who had followed Jesus watched as his body was placed in the tomb. Wiping away their tears, they sadly returned home to prepare ointments and spices for his burial.

At dawn on Sunday morning, Mary Magdalene, Mary the mother of James, and Salome carried their jars of spices and ointments to the tomb. When they arrived, they found the huge stone rolled away and the tomb open. They went in, but Jesus' body was gone!

Suddenly two angels appeared, dressed in shining robes. The frightened women bowed low before them.

"Why do you look here among the dead for one who lives?" the angels asked. "He is not here. He is alive again!"

The joyful women rushed back to Jerusalem to tell the disciples—and everyone else—what had happened. Jesus was alive!

## Match these words with the words in the picture:

| | | |
|---|---|---|
| Tomb | Spice | Ointment |
| Stone | Salome | Mary Magdalene |
| Angel | Robe | Mary the Mother |
| Linen Shroud | Jerusalem | of James |

## Jesus Returns to Heaven

After Jesus' death, the disciples were afraid they too would be killed, so they met secretly behind locked doors.

Mary Magdalene ran breathlessly to their hiding place, pounding on the door until they let her in. "Jesus is alive!" she shouted. But they did not believe her.

Then suddenly, Jesus himself stood among them. They were terribly frightened, for they thought he was a ghost. But Jesus showed them his wounds and asked for food, and at last they believed he was alive. They clapped their hands and laughed for joy.

Later, Peter and the others returned to Galilee, to the Sea of Tiberias. There they began to fish, but they caught nothing. Once more Jesus appeared, calling to them from the beach. Suddenly their nets were full of fish.

Later Jesus told them: "It is written in the scriptures that the Christ should suffer and die and on the third day should rise from the dead."

And the disciples cried, "Yes, Lord, we have seen these things!"

After forty days, Jesus sent his disciples to a mountaintop in Galilee and spoke to them: "I have all power. Therefore I command you, tell all people about me, baptizing them in the name of the Holy Spirit. All who turn to me shall have their sins forgiven. The Holy Spirit will come upon you and you will receive power, just as my Father promised. And remember, I am with you always, even to the end of the age."

Then he rose into heaven, and they saw him no more.

The disciples blinked and rubbed their eyes, bewildered and confused. But then two angels appeared to them in a blinding light. "Why do you stand looking into heaven?" said the angels. "Jesus will come again just as you saw him leave."

And so the disciples, wondering at all the things they had heard and seen, returned to Jerusalem to await the Holy Spirit.

**Match these words with the words in the picture:**

| | | |
|---|---|---|
| Wound | Heaven | Peter |
| Mountaintop | Light | Lord Jesus Christ |
| Angel | Sea of Tiberias | |
| Cloud | Disciple | |

Cloud

Heaven

Lord
Jesus
Christ

Wound

Light

Angel

Peter

Sea of
Tiberias

Mountaintop

Disciple

## To This Day

One day soon after Jesus returned to heaven, people from every nation crowded into Jerusalem to celebrate the joyous festival of Pentecost. The disciples, or apostles, as they were now called, gathered there, too, in an upper room to pray.

Suddenly, the Holy Spirit filled the apostles, and they spoke to the people in many tongues.

The people whispered and buzzed with excitement, for each heard and understood what was spoken in his own language.

About three thousand came to believe in Jesus that day, and from that day to this, people everywhere still believe.